The Happy Mommy Guide: Things-to-do BEFORE & AFTER Becoming a Mommy

The Happy Mommy Guide: Things-to-do BEFORE & AFTER Becoming a Mommy

Jacqi Leyva-Hill, M.ED., MMP

Rev. date: 07/23/2020

To order additional copies of this book, contact:
Xlibris
1-888-795-4274
www.Xlibris.com
Orders@Xlibris.com
772756

CONTENTS

PROLOGUE

Hello Beautiful!

Thank you so much for picking up this book that means so much to me. I wrote this book based on a famous quote by

Frederick Douglass
American Abolitionist

"It is easier to build strong children than to repair broken men."

As I write this book, I have been a mommy for more than eleven years. Once I realized that kids don't need a perfect mommy, they just need a happy mommy, I felt relieved and a new motivation to take control of my emotions better! Now I want to share the lessons I have learned from my own journey and from watching other mommies to empower future mommies and current mommies to create happier families worldwide.

While it is never a bad time to make the decision to be the happiest mommy version of yourself. I do believe that early preparation is key to a happier outcome when it comes to so many things in life. So I hope that if you are preparing to be a mom in the next year or in the next 15 years that you enjoy this compilation of the life's lessons that I have learned by watching others and from making my own mistakes. If you are already a mom, I hope that you can use this book to help you be the happiest mommy possible, so you can raise a happy family of your own starting today. You want to be a happy mommy because a happy mommy is a strong mommy. A happy mommy uses the strength of the Lord as the source of her joy so that she can control her emotions to be able to handle negativity with more ease and grace throughout life.

Habakkuk 3:17-18 ESV

**Though the fig tree should not blossom,
nor fruit on the vines, I will take
joy in the God of my salvation.**

Once I learned that kids don't need a perfect mommy, but they do need a happy one, I have strived to manage my emotions and be the happiest mommy that I could be using my faith in Christ.

James 1:2-4 ESV Count it all joy, my brothers, when you meet trials of various kinds, for you know that the testing of your faith produces steadfastness. And let steadfastness have its full effect, that you may be perfect and complete, lacking in nothing.

Nehemiah 8:10 ESV

**Then he said to them, "Go your way. Eat the
fat and drink sweet wine and send portions
to anyone who has nothing ready, for this day
is holy to our Lord. And do not be grieved,
for the joy of the Lord is your strength.**

CHAPTER 1

Heal Yourself from Your Past
To Prepare for the Future

My dad used to always say to me, "Someone always has it better than you in life, and someone always has it worse than you in life, so be grateful for your problems." I know that sounds cliché, but as I grew older, I found that to be true. My parents divorced when I was 10 and a half, after that it seems that I started to meet a lot of kids like me, searching for meaning only to discover that some of their childhoods had been much rougher than mine, while others had a better childhood or so I thought. Either way though, we were all in pain, and pain is no fun, especially when you are a lost hurt kid.

I grew up attending the Catholic Church but found that even though I knew all of the prayers and did all of the confessions, I still felt unfulfilled, defeated, guilty, and less than worthy to be truly loved. It wasn't until one day that I was watching one of my favorite pastors on tv, at one of my lowest moments in life, and he told the story of what Jesus did for me (and the world) in Hell. When he explained the events, in his own words, of course, leading up to what the scripture meant, it touched my heart and made years of religion all make sense within a single moment in time. I felt a rebirth in my spirit, body and mind immediately after he explained the following scripture and that day I started my personal journey on becoming a born again believer.

Colossians 2:15 (AMP)

When He had disarmed the rulers and authorities [those supernatural forces of evil operating against us], He made a public example of them [exhibiting them as

captives in His triumphal procession], having triumphed over them through the cross.

The pastor talked about how Jesus submitted to death, because of His faith in the Father's love and plan for Him, to be able to defeat the devil so that the devil could not defeat me, as long as I BELIEVED. The pastor described how the devil thought he had to kill Jesus amongst sinners, as if he had been a sinner, but there was a bigger plan on the line that Jesus knew about that included him being tortured and put on the cross, so he submitted to death to free us from hell. In the Bible in the Book of Acts, my pastor went on to explain that Jesus went all the way down to the pangs of death, the very bottom of Hades so that you and I wouldn't have to. Satan thought he won the battle after Jesus breathed his last breathe on Earth.

But my pastor went on to explain that the devil underestimated the power of Christians, and how we don't live our lives based on what it looks like. He gave examples of this by saying "When Mary announced that she was pregnant, it looked like she had been fooling around. When the children of Israel came upon the Red Sea, it looked like they were stuck. When certain bills came into your house, it looked like you weren't going to be handle them. When certain trouble showed up in your life, it looked like you were going to be defeated. But everyone one of us has a testimony of how it looked like you were going down and God came and lifted us up. So we don't live by what it looked like. It may look like you are on your way down now, but the big hand of God is about to show up and deliver you once again out of what it looks like."

COLOSSIANS 2:15 (GNT)

And on that cross Christ freed himself from the power of the spiritual rulers and authorities; he made a public spectacle of them leading them as captives in his victory procession.

At this point, my pastor described how Satan had condemned Jesus under the cloak of a sinner into hell because he had died amongst sinners. But once Jesus was in the depths of hell, Jesus took off his cloak of a sinner that he used as a disguise himself to get into hell, and for the first time ever, LIGHT appeared in Hell as the King of Glory stood in the depths of hell.

My pastor continued to describe in his own unique version of what happened in hell by saying "Jesus began to take them to school and said, 'I looked like I sinned, but I never sinned. Just as you came into my garden (of Eden) illegally, I am here (in hell) illegally and I am here to set the captives free and am going to strip you of your authority right now'

That day Jesus crushed the head of Satan just as it had been prophesized 4000 years earlier to Satan after he caused the fall of Adam and Eve in the beginning:

Genesis 3:15 (AMP)

**And I will put enmity (open hostility)
between you and the woman, and between
your seed and her seed (offspring),
He shall [fatally] bruise your head
and you shall only bruise his heel.**

This sermon CHANGED my life because it donned on me that I was not stuck in an unforgiven state and that I could look up out of the pit of hell that I felt that I was living in and reach out to God who would light the way for me out of the darkness. Jesus saves everyone who believes in Him. That was such GOOD NEWS to me! But just because you understand what Jesus did once and for all, the devil will try to remind of our past to put us in bondage of guilt again and make us lose control of our emotions. So must fight against the devil and meditate daily on the following scriptures to be able to speak them out loud to protect us from regressing back to feeling guilty and hurt from our past. These include Hebrews 8:12, John 3:17,

Ephesians 1:7, Romans 8:1, 2nd Corinthians 5:21 & 5:27.

Later in another sermon my pastor posed the question, "Do you really believe in Jesus?" I thought to myself, "Of course I do! Why would I be watching you if I didn't?" But then he went on to say how so many people fail I their faith because of a lack of belief. When people like this consulted with him, he posed this question to them, and it really made me think. He asked, "What do you think caused the followers of Jesus to go from hiding in an upstairs room away from the Romans to later leave that room and shamelessly proclaim the Gospel of Grace that Jesus taught before he was crucified?" He went to ask, "Do you think the Jews paid them to leave their safe place of hiding to going outside?" I thought to myself, "No way, they just had turned him over to the Romans to be crucified!"

Hebrews 8:12 NLT

And I will forgive their wickedness, and I will never again remember their sins.

John 3:17 NLT

God sent his Son into the world not to judge the world, but to save the world through him.

Ephesians 1:7 NLT

He is so rich in kindness and grace that he purchased our freedom with the blood of his Son and forgave our sins.

Romans 8:1 NLT

So now there is no condemnation for those who belong to Christ Jesus.

2nd Corinthians 5:21 NLT

For God made Christ, who never sinned, to be the offering for our sin, so that we could be made right with God through Christ.

My fave pastor went on to describe how to renew our mind so that we don't fall prey to the devil's lies which lead us into guilt, depression and anger.

These are the things that make us lose control of our emotions and rob us of our happiness.

Proverbs 23:7 KJB

For as a man thinketh in his heart, so is he...

He says that if we find ourselves losing control, we need to get into God's Word so that we can be spiritually minded to have joy and peace. If we find our mind being emotionally ruled (ruled by our 5 senses) and thinking negative thoughts, we must change what we are exposed to because what we are exposed to determines how we feel. Our feelings, he says, determines the decisions that we make. The decisions we make determine our actions, and our actions determine our habits. Our habits determine our character, and our character determines our destination.

As future mommies and current mommies, our ideal destination is for our children to reach adulthood with happy memories and love in their heart for us so that they can live out a healthy happy adulthood.

But if we fill our children's childhood with memories of pain, anger, depression and sadness, they will carry that into their adulthood which will spill into their children's lives. So it is up to us what kind of legacy we leave for our children, as well as our future grandchildren, and it all starts with our mind.

My pastor went on to ask, "Do you think the Romans paid them to leave their hiding space to go out and proclaim the Word of God to the world?" Again, I thought to myself, "Heck no, that is why they crucified Him, to keep him from causing trouble with Cesar, who preferred to be thought of as all powerful." So I pondered the question and watched the movie, "The Bible," and realized that only Jesus coming back and showing His wounds would make the fear of being tortured and crucified go away, only to be replaced with an unwaivering faith. Once they were convinced that

Jesus had conquered death to return and prove who He really was, were they able to leave the room they had been hiding in without fear and proclaim to the world like they did.

So my advice to you, a future mommy, is to first heal yourself by forgiving yourself with the Word of God. Understand that whatever has happened before today is the past and as long as you look up to God and get to know His promises for you, you will start to become a happier and happier person, because God will never fail you.

Find a good Bible-based church that can help you decipher the Word correctly so that you can find healing for the past hurts and disappointments in your life. Or do like I do, and watch your favorite pastors on tv, YouTube, or their app. Whatever you decide, the more Word you get, the more POWER you will have to be happy. Healing yourself will keep you from hurting your future baby, family and friends.

Ephesians 4:31-32 AMP

Get rid of all bitterness, rage, and anger, brawling and slander, along with every form of malice. 32 Be kind and compassionate to one another, Forgiving each other, just as Christ forgave you.

Another one of my favorite pastors on tv is a woman who was severely sexually abused from very early in her life. To hear her tell the tale of her childhood sounds like a nightmare that not even Hollywood has seen. But she found God, learned about His son Jesus and what was accomplished during the three days of him publicly dying on the cross, and was able to not only forgive her parents, but actually help her to provide for her parents in their last days very handsomely.

To tell you the truth, I don't know how a person survives abuse like that and then turns around and forgives unconditionally, but after I got deeper in my faith with Jesus, I realized that it was because of what Jesus did, that she was able to do that.

Using Jesus' strength, not hers alone, was how she was able to be so strong. Now she lives an amazing, peaceful, and prosperous life teaching others about God's grace.

Luke 10:19 (AMP)

Listen carefully: I have given you authority [that you now possess] To tread on serpents and scorpions, and [the ability to exercise authority] over all the power of the enemy (Satan); And nothing will [in any way], harm you.

So I implore you, that no matter what stage you are in right now in life, start to heal yourself with Jesus's strength and not your own. Now, I do protect myself from people with toxic energy from infecting my life, but I can honestly say that I do love them from afar because when I think of how Jesus was publicly tortured and put to an earthly death, I think to myself, "Well, at least those people did not do that to me, so I have to forgive like Jesus did."

Perspective is everything. My favorite pastor says that when you find yourself feeling down and depressed because of what has happened to you in the past, you need to take control of your emotions. He calls it the Anatomy of Life. If you don't like how you are feeling, change what you are thinking about. If you don't like what you are thinking about, change what you are exposing yourself to.

For example, if you watch a lot of tv, you will find yourself feeling depressed because you may think everyone has it better than you in life, which is simply not true. Media has a way of making us feel like we need their advertiser's products to be pretty enough, skinny enough, wealthy enough, etc. But the reality is that when the producer yells 'Cut!" then the actors return to their real lives and not everything they do is for show.

If you watch documentaries about formerly famous actors when they were growing up, you find out that a lot of the time that they were on tv or the big screen with a big smile on their face, the whole time off the set their life was a nightmare beyond most of our imaginations. (Think about the stories of Whitney Houston, Corey Feldman and Corey Haim, for example). So limit your viewing of fruitless tv and big screen shows that show lots of sex and violence mixed with images of a glamorous life because you may get caught up in trying to achieve a ficticious make believe life, that won't be good for you, your baby, family or friends.

I realize that some of my readers may be from different walks in their spiritual life, but when I realized that of all the great spiritual leaders, Jesus was the only one who conquered death and came back to prove he was still spiritually alive after a public execution, I had to make him my Lord and Savior.

If you are scared to believe because you feel guilty for things that you may have done or felt in your past, don't worry, there is no unforgiveable sin, except for the sin of unbelief. If you don't believe in what Jesus did, then you cannot receive His blessing and grace in your life. So go ahead, ponder the question and really get into your heart and mind the spirit of belief. I promise that once you have it, you will grow in your relationship with God and receive what you really want to receive in life.

Matthew 7:7 AMP

Ask and keep on asking and it will be given to you; seek and keep on seeking and you will find; knock and keep on knocking and the door will be Opened to you.

You may be wondering why this is the first thing that I recommend to you do at this point, and I will tell you why. Because hurt people hurt people most of the time. We are all born angels of God sent to our parents to discover our life's purpose and that is where we learn how to treat others. So if we are taught hate, violence, greed, or any other negative behavior, then that is what we give to every person we meet. It takes a conscious decision to not be a reflection of what negative earthly family members and people around us have shown us, but rather to be a reflection of God's goodness, and that takes faith. Before becoming a mommy, or if you are already a mommy, I recommend that you get an understanding of how divinely you are made and the authority on Earth that we have been given to create a great life for yourself and your future family. Know that God Loves You and He made you in His image.

Genesis 2:27 (NAB)

God created man in his image;
In the divine image he created him;
male and female he created them.

Psalm 139: 13-14 (AMP)

13 For You formed my innermost
parts; You knit me
[together] in my mother's womb.
14 I will give thanks and
praise to You, for I am
Fearfully and wonderfully made;

**Wonderful are your works, And
my soul knows it very well.**

Lastly, make sure that you meditate on God's Word to know God's will for your life. Don't be deceived by the world in thinking that the world's way is a good way to live your life by.

Isaiah 5:20-21(NLT)

**What sorrow for those who say that
evil is good and good is evil, that
dark is light and light is dark, that
bitter is sweet and sweet is bitter.
21 What sorrow for those who are wise in
their own eyes and think themselves so clever.**

CHAPTER 2

Figure Out Who You Are and What Kind of Mom That You Want to Be

So now that you understand why it is important to heal from your past hurts, it is time believe that you are loved. Being a happy mommy means believing that YOUR ARE LOVED.

1 John 4:19 (NAB)

We love because he first loved us.

Love is the only thing that always wins. Because you are loved, you have been given authority to become the kind of mom that you want to be going forward. Know that God loves you and as long as you stay connected to Him in your heart and your mind, you will be able to create the future you want for you and your future family. We have been given authority as believers and only you can choose to use it. Your future baby and family does not have to be abused and impoverished because we have been given authority over disease and demons.

Matthew 10:1 (NAB)

**Then he summoned his twelve disciples
and gave them authority over
Unclean spirits to drive them out and to
cure every disease and every illness.**

So now that you can see that you have the authority to create the kind of future you want for you and your future family, envision the kind of mom that you want to be. I believe that everything is made twice, once in your mind, then in reality. You have the power to create a healthy and happy family. Do you want to be a stay at home mommy? Do you want to be instrumental in teaching your future baby about life, love and relationships or do you envision yourself to be more hands off? Either way, you want to be in control of your situation and what your future baby is exposed to.

Don't worry about being perfect, just make sure that you are happy. The easiest way to do that is to stay thankful to fill yourself with the joy of the Lord.

Psalm 28:7 (AMP)

**The Lord is my strength and my
[impenetratable] shield;
My heart trusts [with unwavering
confidence] in Him, and
I am helped; Therefore my
heart greatly rejoices,
And with my song I shall thank
Him and praise Him.**

At this point, you may feel like your upbringing was so devoid of true unconditional love that you are not able to give it because you did not receive it. But I will reassure you that as long as you intentionally stay in the Word of God and believe that God Loves You, you will be happier and be able to give love to your future baby. If there are negative or toxic people in your family or circle of friends, you will want to plan now to be able to put some space between you and them so that your future baby and family does not fall victim to them.

Ephesians 6:11 AMP

**Put on the full armor of God [for
His precepts are like the splendid
Armor of a heavily armored soldier], so that
you may be able to [successfully] stand up
against all schemes and the strategies and the
Deceits of the devil.**

My favorite pastor uses the analogy of the electric company to demonstrate the power we have been given and the ability we have to use it to be a happy mommy. As customers of the electric company, we are given electricity into our homes, but if we want light in a room, we have to flip the switch. The electric company does not come out to flip the switch in each room for us, they just supply the power to us. So, as a believer, you are given the power and authority to be a happy mom, but you have to decide that you want to flip the switch, so to say, and then FLIP THE SWITCH.

Finally, I encourage you to discover your "love language" to help improve your communication with your loved ones. According to Gary Chapman, the author of "The Five Love Languages: How to Express Heartfelt Commitment to Your Mate," which was written for your mate, but I think it is good to understand all of your loved ones' love language. Communication is key to attaining a good relationship with anybody.

As summarized by Wikipedia, the five ways to express and experience love that Chapman calls "loved languages" are:
1. by giving and receiving words of affirmation
2. by giving and receiving quality of time
3. by giving and receiving gifts

4. by doing and receiving acts of service

5. by giving and receiving physical touch.

He suggests that everyone has a primary and secondary preference of showing love and we need to observe our loved ones requests and complaints to understand their love language.

Knowledge is power, the more you know about yourself and others, the more you grow.

CHAPTER 3

Save, Budget, and Invest to Get Financially Fit!

This is a very important step because this is about achieving your FINANCIAL FREEDOM to be a happy mommy. You may not think that is important, but it is because many women caught in abusive relationships feel stuck because of their financial situation. So figuring out how money works, how you can earn it with ease and how to invest for your future emergency needs is vital to becoming a happy mommy.

The first step in financial freedom is finding out who you are and what you want to be in life. It is best to do this step BEFORE becoming a mommy, but if you are already a mommy, then today is the best day to take this step. Ask yourself, "If money was not important, what would I want to work at in life?" Journal about what makes you happy. Are you happiest when you are cooking? Are you happiest when you are outside in the garden? Are you happiest when you are apart of a group working on a project? Are you happiest doing research? Then do what makes you happy.

If you don't know what makes you happy, then you need to get in God's Word to give you confidence to try new things in life and step out of your comfort zone. The devil will try to deceive you and make you think that you are not good enough to become what you dream to be, but God tells you in His Word that you are beautifully and miraculously made for a purpose. Don't rush through this step, really take time to discover that purpose that drives your passion up in life.

Ecclesiastes 3: 1 (AMP)

There is a season [a time appointed] for everything and a time for every delight And event or purpose under heaven

How will you know when you have found your passion in life? When you can get out of bed in the morning before the alarm clock goes off to start your day with a sense of joy and not dread. Life is about work. You have to work at being happy. You have to work at being sad. That statement might make you uncomfortable, but it is true. You have to work at keeping control of your emotions so that you can feel happy. People unknowingly work at being sad when they listen to the negative voices from the people around them that have been planted in their head. You can take control of your emotions if you refer back to the God's promise for your life.

Phillippians 2:13 (NAB)

For God is the one who, for his good purpose, Works in you both to desire and to work.

I believe each human being was given special God-given talents that need to be developed, to be a a happy mommy. To be financially fit, you have to understand money, so you need to take steps and enroll in classes on Income Tax, Real Estate (first home ownership and investing), Securities and Insurance. These classes are available online and on site more and more all of the time. Some of these classes are available through schools and others through businesses like H & R Block, which is where I learned about income taxes. We listen to the Rich Dad Radio Show to learn about current topics in the financial world amongst other YouTube channels.

At this point, I do have to emphasize that I do not believe that money buys anyone happiness, but it does buy you choices and options. Without money, your choices and options are limited. You want to have many options and choices when you become a happy mommy so that you are not frustrated. Frustrated and cranky mommies are more apt to do things that are harmful to themselves and their families. Drugs and alcohol abuse usually occurs when people want to escape a situation but feel stuck and helpless. Mommies endanger themselves and their baby (or babies) when they feel like they have no choice but to put up with a bad situation of abuse or neglect.

2 Corinthians 8:9 (AMP)

**For you are recognizing [more clearly]
the grace of our Lord Jesus Christ
{His astonishing kindness, His
generosity, His gracious favor], that
Though he was rich, yet for your sake he
became poor, so that by His poverty
You might become rich [abundantly blessed].**

So with that said, the first thing that I recommend is to buy a whole life insurance policy when you start earning money as soon as you can. Why? Because life insurance is cheap when you are healthy and young. Even Robert Kiyosaki, author of the book, "Rich Dad, Poor Dad,' has wrote about the benefits of having a whole life policies to build up cash values. These cash values can be used for EMERGENCY NEEDS that you can use without penalty for any reason you feel you need your money. Of course, the longer you let the money grow, the richer you will be, so it is best to have more than one in your name because no one can steal the money from you.

These kinds of policies act like a super savings account for you and grow without being taxed as long as you keep the policy in force. Every time that you pay for your policy, a portion of that amount [the premium] goes towards a savings account that earns interest and grows money for you to use without having to qualify for it. And if you do pass away early, they will be provided for and not a burden on another family to care for. Another option is to have a Return of Premium term insurance, aka Cash Back Option, so that at the end of the term, (10,20,or 30 years) you get your money back if you didn't die. These are great as a type of "forced savings account" and can even help you pay your mortgage off faster if structured correctly.

Proverbs 13:22 AMP

**A good man leaves an inheritance
[of moral stability and goodness]
to his children's children,
And the wealth of the sinner [finds
its way eventually] into the hands
Of the righteous, for whom It was laid up**

If you build up cash values in your home, called home equity, and want to access it, the bank will pull your credit report to make sure you have a history of paying money back. That does not happen when you call your whole life insurance policy company and ask to have your cash values sent to you wherever you may be at. This is a very valuable money tool to get when you are young and healthy so that you always have options and choices to get you unstuck should you find yourself in a bad situation.

Trust me, it is not if anything ever goes wrong in life, it is WHEN things go wrong in life, you want to be able to be in control of the situation rather than let your negative emotions control you at these points in your life and having an extra account of cash money can help you take control of a situation.

The second thing that I would say to do is figure out how much you need in savings or passive income to be able to stay home and raise your baby. I have never met a mom who wanted to leave her baby to go earn a living and miss out on all of the important moments of being a mommy. Work will always be available, just like the party life, but your children are only little for a little while. Then they grow up and leave you to live their own lives.

Financial education is key to you being a happy mommy, and I cannot over stress that point to you. If you look at women in abusive situations and in battered women's shelter, you will find women who have very little or no financial education that can improve their life's circumstances. This book aims to deplete the shelters of abused women and children by empowering future mommies and current moomies on how to do life God's way, because is the most prosperous way. My goal is empower mommies and their families to be safe and secure, not impoverished and abused. People who don't understand money may make fun of you and try to deceive you that you are not smart enough, but you are. Ask question, seek knowledge from those that you want to emulate in life. Know that Jesus came to give us an abundant life.

John 10:10 (NAB)

A thief comes only to steal and slaughter and destroy; I came so that they might have life and have it more abundantly.

CHAPTER 4

Love Thy Body, Love Thy Self

Self esteem is so important to becoming a happy mommy. If you are always comparing yourself to photoshopped images of women, then you will feel bad about yourself and not be happy. And again I say, a child does not need a perfect mommy, but they do need a happy mommy to grow up into happy adults in life.

So if you don't love yourself, you will endanger your future baby. Again, some women punish themselves with pills, alcohol, dangerous diets and other extremes to punish themselves for being who they are. So if there is something that you do not like about yourself physically, come to an understanding that there are people in the world who would love to look like you and be able to do what you can do.

When you look in the mirror, meditate on this scripture:

Ecclesiastes 3:11 (AMP)

**He has made everything beautiful
and appropriate in its time.**

My professional background is in medical massage therapy and personal training along with teaching fitness classes, so I know the pain of women trying to change their bodies with and without surgeries. My advice to anyone considering having plastic surgery done, do it before becoming a mommy. One of the saddest stories that I ever heard of was of a young mom who went in to have her breasts augmented who died on the operating table leaving behind her 7 year old little boy. I can only imagine that her child did not care that his mommy was not a full bra cup, but that he had a mommy. That day, after he got out of school, he discovered that he had lost and that is such a painful of a story to me.

Of course there is never a good time to pass away on an operating table, but at least if you did not have children depending on you, for love and a livelihood, it would be less tragic. With different innovations in weight loss now, that don't require you to go under the knife to get results, like bodywraps, along with compression garments and of course a sensible diet used in combination with exercise, there are ways to improve your body without going under the knife.

Nevertheless, it is important to feel good about yourself. When i used to teach modeling school, I would instruct the girls to find a model or actress that they admired that had the same body type as they had. Nowadays, there are all kinds of body types that are celebrated in the media. Never the less it is important to exercise regularly, like every other day at least for 30 minutes. Dance, walk, jog, ride a bike, take a weight training class, try pilates and yoga to keep yourself strong. Strong is sexy. Sexy makes us feel desireable and that is what a healthy mommy should strive for. I have done research on waist trainers and compression garments and have found they are very effective at helping us attain the shape that we want to be when combined with diet and exercise. You will want to create a healthy body image and a healthy eating plus exercise routine especially before becoming a mommy so that when your body takes on a bigger shape, you will know how to put yourself back together relatively quickly. But again, I reiterate, TODAY is the best day to start on the road to being a happy mommy.

1 Corinthians 6:19 AMP

Do you not know that your body is a temple of the Holy Spirit who is within you, Whom you have [received as a gift] from God, and that you are not your own property?

Being at peace with yourself will help you to be a happy mommy with a radiant glow that your family and friends will love about you. You can't assume anyone will love you if you don't love yourself, though your children will. Unfortunately, mommies who don't value and honor themselves usually end up disrespecting themselves and their children, which is not God's best for our lives. So be the best version of what God thought you up to be.

1 Corinthians 6:20 AMP

20 You were bought with a price of[you were actually purchased with The precious blood of Jesus and made His own],. So then Honor and Glorify God with Your Body

CHAPTER 5

Use the Magic of the 30-second Hug Every Day in Your Life

We as humans are electrical-chemical machines. Our heart runs on electrical impulses and body is influenced heavily by our hormones. As humans, we crave to be loved and to love others. However, because love has been confused with abuse in negative relationships, people find themselves devoid of being hugged and of wanting to hug others.

But we are also energy fields of frequencies because we are more than just a body, we are a spirit that owns a soul. Our soul is our mind, our emotions, and our feelings. We can elevate ourselves and can be lifted up to feel closer to God, and we should do that frequently throughout the day. One way to do that starting today is to give your loved ones, whomever they should be, intentional, heart-to-heart 30-second hugs along with a kiss on the cheek to get into the good habit to become a happy mommy.

These kinds of intentional heart-to-heart hugs with a kiss release oxytocin in the brain, which is your bonding hormone. Sometimes when we are tired or stressed, we give half- hearted hugs to our loved ones and they don't benefit us or them as much as they could if they were held intentionally for thirty seconds.

Sharing and bonding regularly and frequently creates a peace in the body and mind that can help fight off dis-ease that leads to disease, illness and negative behavior bouts. Try it and see!

1 Peter 5:14 AMP

**Greet one another with a kiss
of love. To all of you
who are in Christ, may there be peace.**

Also, remember to be aware of your surroundings and protect yourself from people with bad vibrations or frequencies. If you don't know what that means, think back to a time when you met someone whom you had never met before and for no reason at all, there was an instant happy feeling, almost as if ya'll had been good friends before meeting that day. That is an example of a person with good vibrations that resonated with your own. Now think back to a time when you met someone for the first time, and for no specific reason, ya'll repelled each other, as if there was some bad blood, so to say, from the past. That would be an example of someone with toxic or low vibrations that did not resonate with you. Never ignore your Holy Spirit trying to guide you. Many people call it their gut instinct, but as you grow in your relationship with God, you will come to realize that it is the Holy Spirit speaking to you.

I bring this up because, especially as a mommy, you want to be in tune with the Holy Spirit guiding you to the people and places that you will thrive in. Some people refer to this phenomena as 'listening to their gut." If you ever listen to women's stories of past abuse, more times than not they will speak of a bad feeling in their 'gut' that they ignored, that somehow ended putting them or their children in danger. I implore you to get spiritually minded so that you can be attentive to signs that will help you and your family avoid danger.

CONCLUSION

And with that, I will conclude this book. I hope that I have inspired you to seek God wholeheartedly and to discover His promises for yourself in the Bible so that you know in your heart that His Word is truth. If you were wondering who my favorite pastor is that I kept referencing throughout the book, it is Creflo Dollar. If you are wondering who my favorite female pastor is who I referred to as well, it is Joyce Meyers. If you have never been exposed to the Word filled with hope, I recommend starting out with another one of my favorite pastors, Joel Osteen, and then find yourself a good Bible-based church. Like I said before, I do all of my Bible studies online and on tv, following along in the Good Book (the Bible) since none of my favorites live in my town. Constantly fill yourself up now with the joy of the Lord, day and night. Highlight your Bible and know where to find the scriptures that pertain to your situation in life. Know that you are loved by God at all times and He will never leave or fail you like human beings can do (they die, get lost on the way home from the store, etc.) Remember, no kid needs a perfect mom, they just need a happy mom that will lead them to a relationship with God to see them through the rough times that are undoubtedly apart of life.

Jeremiah 29:11-13 AMP

For I know the plans and thoughts that I have for you," says the Lord, "plans For peace and well-being and not for disaster, to give you a future and a hope. 12 Then you will call on me and you will come and pray to Me, and I will

Hear [your voice] and I will listen to you. 13 Then [with a deep longing] you will seek Me and require Me [as a vital necessity] and [you will] find Me when you search for Me With all of your heart.

BIOGRAPHY

Jacqueline Leyva-Hill aka "Jacqi Hill", is a native of San Antonio, Texas and was awarded the Ms. Photogenic at the 1998 Miss Latina USA. She became the wife of Albert Hill in 2005 and became the mother to one son, J.R. Hill in 2008. She is the winner of the Mrs. Petite United America 2013 title and loves being a wife and mom. She has an undergraduate degree in Health and a graduate degree in Exercise Science since 1995 and she is a patented inventor. Jacqi has written health and fitness articles for several magazines including "Enjoy Whole Health," and "Street Talk" in San Antonio, Texas. She currently works as a Health and Wellness Coach and is currently a Life and Health insurance agent in the financial industry.

Jacqi started to explore her spirituality in Los Angeles, CA when she lived there for 8 years, during which time she got married and had her son. She enlisted in the Universal Church as a pastor as far back as the early 2000's when she first arrived on Venice Beach, CA.

The insights shared in this book have all come from her own prayerful life and the work that she has done volunteering with a local foster child organization. After seeing first-hand how girls who are not prepared to have babies usually ended up abusing and abandoning them, Jacqi chose to write this book to help future families of America and around the world.

Jacqi manages a few social media pages on Facebook including the Wise Moms and Glammas of SA page and her Health, Wealth, Love, and Beauty page. Her business page, Jacqi's Nu Fitness, showcases her current work and her YouTube channel, Jacqi Hill, has just been started up since the quarantine.

Jacqi also worked with women of all ages for over 25 years as a personal trainer, fitness instructor and massage therapist.

To reach Jacqi, you can email her at <u>jacqi27@ icloud.com</u> or text directly to her business cell at 210-410-0325.